The Art of Appliqué

Marie-Janine Solvit

ARCO PUBLISHING, INC.
215 Park Avenue South, New York, NY 10003

Above: *Chica. Study in blues and greens, enlivened by their complementary colours.*

Page 1: *Janna Drake. Very beautiful monochrome study in autumnal colours, of which velvet is a major ingredient. The sky is hand-painted on a plain background.*

Front cover: *Silk appliqué by J. Le Voyer.*
Back cover: *Old mola, author's collection. Picture by Maryvonne Breitenstein.*

Published 1984 by Arco Publishing, Inc.
215 Park Avenue South, New York, NY 10003

Originally published in France under the title *Les appliqués*.
Copyright © 1980 Dessain et Tolra.

Translated by M. S. Rohan.

English edition copyright © 1982 EP Publishing Limited.
Printed and bound in Italy.

Library of Congress Cataloging in Publication Data

Solvit, Marie Janine.
  The art of appliqué.

  Translation of: Les appliqués.
  1. Appliqué. I. Title.
TT779.S65 1984 - 746.44'5 - 84-3063
ISBN 0-668-06243-6 (pbk.)

Picture credits

Maryvonne Breitenstein: pp. 16, 24, 25, 26, 39, 49 (right), 50, 60. Pierre-Gilles Solvit: pp. 1, 2, 5, 18, 19, 20, 23, 27 to 32 (top), 34, 37, 38, 41 to 48, 49 (top), 51, 53, 54, 56, 58, 59, 61 (bottom), 62, 63, 64. Musée de l'Homme, Paris: pp. 6 (top), 12, 14 (bottom). José Oster collection: pp. 10 (bottom), 13. Daniel Ponsard collection: 6 (bottom), 7 to 9, 10 (top). Destable collection: p. 15. Musée des Arts Decoratifs, Paris: p. 11. The photograph at the top of page 61 was published by kind permission of Mme. Sophie Campbell, teacher of patchwork. The other pieces were kindly lent by their creators. Sketches by the author.

Contents

*Michèle Bedel de Raffin.
Private collection. This richly
complex composition is made
up of silks and flowers cut
out from floral prints.*

Chica. A breath of fresh air. . . Humour and the unexpected in motion. Very small 'dabs' of fabric.

What is appliqué?

One element stitched onto another base element. You could say, for example, that the simplest forms are the sewn-on patch pocket and the leather reinforcement patches at elbow and shoulder so dear to the British tweed jacket.

I would like to be your guide on a voyage of exploration around the world of appliqué. The principal basic styles, their inspirations and their *raisons d'être* will lead us on to encounter a new contemporary craft style, a melting-pot of traditional techniques. Creative imagination, freed from traditional constraints but enriched by their example, is bringing a fresh breath of life to the craft we shall be studying together—the very ancient but still lively technique of appliqué.

After this, we will take a closer look at the steps in preparing, executing and finishing appliqué pieces of the most widespread and familiar kind—those born in 18th-century North America and belonging to the group generally known as patchwork.

And to round off our studies we shall be admiring some challenging contemporary work.

Back of a bridal robe. Appliqué designs in salmon skin. Ghiliak peoples, Siberia.

Szür in white homespun, Hungary.

Around the world in traditional appliqué

Sophisticated designs and complex creations demanding unshakeable patience are part of the cultural heritage of every country in the world, and especially the least rich. We will be discovering them in Europe, Benin, Afghanistan, Panama, the Hawaiian islands, India and North America.

Siberia

Taking Europe as our starting point and travelling from north to south, we first come across a strange and very artistic use of salmon skin. In Siberia worked fish-skin is actually used to decorate bridal gowns. This one comes from the Amur region of Eastern Siberia, made by the Ghiliak people. The design is symbolic—the tree of life bearing fledglings, symbolizing the children to be born. The most beautiful skin is that of Kumza salmon, from which the superb appliqués we see here are made.

Shoes and hunters' leggings are done in pike-skin, which is the most hardwearing.

Central Europe

Going south from Siberia, we shall see how wool and sheepskin are transformed into rich garments for both men and women—the former decked out like gorgeous birds to go courting, the latter to respond to it with that feminine coquetterie which always seems able to assert itself, even when reduced to herding sheep and coping with crude poverty.

We are in Hungary. These multicoloured garments were once the everyday dress of shepherds in Central Europe of the 19th century, and they are still worn on holidays and special occasions. This characteristically Hungarian man's coat, called a *szür*, was originally embroidered. Then, in the second half of the 19th century, after the appearance of the sewing machine, embroidery was replaced by appliqué. Here we see an example of the *szür* in white homespun adorned with appliqué patches. The coat was generally worn draped across the shoulders, the sleeves left empty. The other *szür* comes from the Sokác people, Catholic Slavs of the Baranya district of Transdanubia, southern Hungary.

Next is the most precious item of a Hungarian woman's costume in the 18th and 19th centuries. Called a *ködmön*, it is made of sheepskin decorated with appliqué patches. It was made by Hungarian furriers known as *Szücs*. Worn by young women with very bright appliqués and by the less young with darker colours, this waistcoat gradually changed style over the years, its appliqués replaced by silk embroidery and then by wool. Unfortunately the breed of Hungarian sheep which yielded such durable skins no longer exists. It has been replaced by merinos, whose thin skin will not stand up to the piercing of an embroiderer's needle. Because of this the garment has become very rare, but is still worn on special occasions. In the photos we can see an original *ködmön* from the Somogy district of Transdanubia, and a second, gaudy with thousands of sheepskin patches, from the village of Szalanta, in the Baranya district of Transdanubia. It is a young Sokác woman's waistcoat.

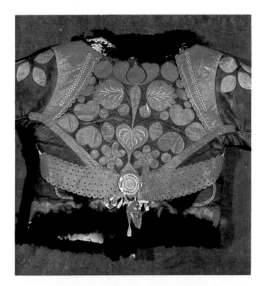

Hungary. Top to bottom:
White homespun szür. Sokác peoples, Transdanubia, Baranya district.
Sheepskin ködmön, Transdanubia, Somogy district.
Young Sokác woman's ködmön, Transdanubia, Baranya district.

7

White tulle tablecloth with linen appliqué.
Calico tablecloth.
Somogy district of Hungary.

Transylvanian szür
Early 20th century

We cannot leave Hungary without admiring these two marvellous appliqué pieces made relatively recently in the village of Buzai, in the Somogy district of Transdanubia. The first is a white tulle tablecloth with appliqués of white linen. The picture shows a quarter of the whole piece. I leave you to contemplate the perfection of it! The second, more rustic in style, is a white calico tablecloth with appliqué decoration in red calico.

We come now to a *szür* from the beginning of this century. Worn by the men of Kalotaszentkirály, in Transylvania, it was made by the Hungarian tailors of Oradéa (Nagyvarad). The craftsmen who made the *szür* were organized into guilds in the towns. Every self-respecting youngster had to have his *szür* to go courting the girls in!

Moving southwards to Rumania, we find there this man's sheepskin jacket; tiny pieces of mirror show through the perforated leather appliqués, held in place by the stitching that secures each piece onto the base. Look at the marvellous design of the sleeve, ending in a strip and cuff of warm black sheepskin which sets off the colours of the pattern.

Here is the waistcoat of a young girl from the Banat district, still worn on special occasions. The skin has been left its curly fleece, and the inside, now the outside, has been entirely covered with appliqué patches; some of them are little circles of leather attached at the centre, making them look like buttons. However, they are only leather cutouts. The garment is called a *cojocel*.

Cojocel from the Banat area of Romania.

*Man's sheepskin jacket, from Romania.
Sleeve and back detail.*

Iberian peninsula

Turning both west and southwards, we come to this *capa de honra*, or cape of honour, from the province of Tras-Os-Montes, in the Braganza district of Portugal. In brown homespun decorated with black and brown cloth appliqué, it bears the date 1926. This noticeably heavy cape is still worn today by heads of families or village elders at meetings of the municipal council.

We continue our European tour in Spain. This peasant-girl's costume from Salamanca, worn on occasion at the beginning of this century, consists of a skirt and halter with appliqué designs on a red ground, an apron with a black background, and a blouse and skirt with black appliqué over a white ground. The skirt and halter are fringed with scalloped cut-outs, and the appliqué elements are linked by embroidery.

France

Our last stop in Europe is France, where appliqué was popular in the last century. Its technique demanded much attention to detail and precision in preparation and execution; it remained faithful in the smallest details to the very ancient technique known as *broderie-appliqué*, already known as long ago as the Middle Ages. The fabrics for appliqué were first glued—and dried in a press to remove any air bubbles—onto very thin paper to which they adhered uniformly, making it easy to cut them out very precisely to a pattern drawn on the back of it. The scissors had to cut without the slightest irregularity because the cloth could never be allowed to fray. The patches thus prepared were then stuck down again onto a chosen background—quickly, so the whole work could be pressed at once. Once completely dry, the appliqués were secured to the background, at first by overcast stitches.

Top: *Capa de Honra. Portugal, Tras-Os-Montes province.*

Bottom: *Spanish peasant girl's costume, Salamanca district.*

Opposite page: *Valance, made in 1883 by Penon after a design by C. Rossigneux. Taffeta appliqués on a woollen backcloth, surrounded by cording and picked out in embroidery in multi-coloured silks.*

Then the fixing process could begin, either:
With piping fixed along the borders between appliqué and background, or with concealed stitches, or with visible embroidery stitches, punctuating the design with small regular touches of colour;
Or with embroidery in satin stitch; all the threads, laid one against the other across where the two pieces of fabric met, had to be strictly the same length.

Another appliqué technique uses patches of leather, Danish hide, especially popular for chair decoration, and Swedish hide, much thinner, for light flexible objects—spectacle cases, portfolios, notecases and so on. It involved fixing them to the background with a backstitch through the patch 1 or 2 mm in from the edge, allowing the thick thread used to 'underline' the design with regular dots.

I cannot leave this section without mentioning the use of cording. This is found, in particular, on rich 18th-century chair-covers. The strips can be narrow or wide. The wider they are, the more tacking is needed to hold them in place. The design, traced onto the backcloth, is thus covered over with strips backstitched on (as unobtrusively as possible). To take in the curves of the design, one must first fix down the outer edge of the strip, then fold the inner edge before sewing to gather in the excess material. Very classically inspired pieces done in this technique contain strips of all sizes, from fine to very broad, and are often augmented with embroidery decorating the areas encircled by the strips.

Fon hanging, in cotton.
The coconut harvest.

Benin

The Fons were a people of ancient Dahomey. Oddly enough, among this agrarian people it was the men who spun the cotton and made lively, naive and colourful wall-hangings, in which people, animals or mythological symbols stand out in blazing colours against a black ground. In the distant past these appliqué pieces were used to decorate royal robes, hangings and ceremonial parasols. We know of royal emblems going back to around 1600. One king would have a fish as emblem, another a bird, a wild pig, a lion or a modest pineapple. To these typical motifs were added scenes in which people fought with great sidearms or muskets. Around 1850 the people of the land clashed in bloody civil wars, and tradition demanded human sacrifices at great ceremonies or the death of a king.

The memory of these massacres still haunts Fon appliqué hangings, but now they are made by professionals working chiefly to satisfy European or American taste for the exotic. The traditional motifs of the ancient art are still used. Drawn on paper templates, they are hemstitched piece by piece onto the indispensable black background. The lighter-skinned people are Fons; darker skins are reserved for their enemies. The style is primitive, spontaneous, and enormously vigorous.

Benin, Abomey region.
Detail from a large cotton wall-hanging. Appliqués in silk and
muslin.
Warriors with cutlasses chopping off the right legs of their
enemies.

Afghanistan

The *gul* is a round appliqué patch in which beads are sewn in adjoining and concentric circles to form rosette patterns. The women of Eastern Afghanistan use them to enhance the embroideries with which their costumes and accessories are decorated. The base fabric of these *guls* is cotton, but is invisible under the beads covering the whole surface. The patterns are regular, and their colour schemes most often include blacks, dark blues or plum colours against which the curving designs are picked out in blues, blue-whites and turquoise blues. The beads are first stitched into the centre of the *gul*, then the lines of the design are traced out in light-coloured thread on the cotton base and the circles expand from the centre out towards the edge. The colour of each bead is determined by its position, on or between the threads tracing out the rosette design.

These *guls* are patched onto embroideries into which little round mirrors are incorporated, which we shall be talking about later. Superimposing these motifs gives the whole a rather overburdened look. But these outfits, in which the circle is the principal decorative element, do not fail to convey an impression of richness and love of detail in the careful embellishment of the most everyday garment.

India and Pakistan

In this part of the world there is a kind of appliqué technique whose speciality is the use of little pieces of mirror, fixed onto the backcloth by embroidery around them. This is *shisha*, also known as 'mirror-embroidery'. The appliqués are called *shishas*. These techniques are chiefly used in a region of Pakistan called

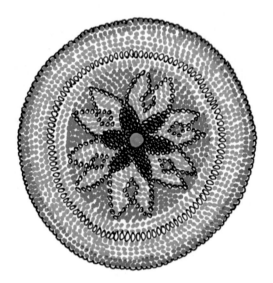

Typical Afghan gul *pattern.*

Border of a guyar *dress, from Rajasthan Barmer.*
The little mirrors can be seen sparkling.

14

Baluchistan. Originally they made use of mirror fragments from glass globes blown by mouth and silvered inside. Jinns and other evil spirits were thus supposed to be frightened away by the sight of their own faces in these little 'witches' mirrors'. From this tradition has survived a glittering appliqué style using little circles of glass or metal over which the embroiderers make a network of threads, afterwards drawn back to the edge by buttonhole stitching to make a coloured surround to the mirror.

In recent years massive importing of *shisha* appliqué work has created a new vogue for these dresses, coats and bags with thousands of sparkling facets. Their days of banishing evil spirits may be past, but they still have power enough to banish dreariness in dress. And dreariness, to my mind, is evil enough to be going on with!

Above you will see a detail from a satin bodice with mirror appliqué, and to the left the border of a *gujar* dress from Rajasthan Barmer. *Gujar* women are generally herdswomen. What a lesson in taste for our own affluent societies!

Rajasthan Barmer. Detail of an embroidered bodice, picked out with shisha *appliqué. (Silk on silk satin.)*

Old mola *from Panama. Author's collection.*

Panama

Molas are appliqué works in a very distinctive style, made by the women of the Cuna tribe, living in southern Central America, in Panama and the neighbouring islands. Until the arrival of French colonists, who imported the idea of clothing, the natives 'dressed' by decorating their skins. Even today the last traces of this very ancient body-painting style survive in a long black vertical line, dividing the faces of some women from the lower forehead to the end of the nose. The Cunas transferred their old skin designs to their clothes, which is why *molas* date only from the middle of the 19th century. Unfortunately the local climate and sunlight conspire to rot and discolour cotton fabrics; appliqué pieces that have survived for thirty years are already considered 'antique'. And antique *molas* are almost undiscoverable.

These sketches show four typical designs, with their maze-like motifs whose lines you seem able to trace out without lifting your hand. The *mola* is made by inlaying and overlaying several cotton cloths of different colours, with which simple appliqués are made. In reverse appliqué technique the design is cut out of the backcloth, and a fabric of a contrasting colour sewn in behind the opening. Straightforward appliqué is also used, in which the appliqué patches are hemstitched onto a backing. In inlay technique the piece is sewn like an ordinary appliqué patch into the cutaway outline of a reverse appliqué. The mixture of these three techniques gives this effect of designs 'underlined' with several lines of different colours, expanding the outline of the main motif outwards from the centre, like contour lines on a map. Each line belongs to a thickness of cloth added over or under the base of the piece. All the outlines are secured with hemstitch.

In addition to their slightly faded 'lived-in' charm, the very oldest *molas* may be recognised by the narrowness of their coloured bands, each one surrounding the one before; and the more recent *molas* can be recognised by the way these coloured areas have become wider! Many themes have inspired the designs—seascapes full of coral reefs; religious motifs from the Pap Ikala faith, with monsters and demons, and Christian motifs as well; animals, birds (eagles, two-headed snake-eating birds), trees and flowers; and also maternal themes, with baby animals around their mother, or shown inside her body.

Typical mola *motifs.*

To use this technique one or two basic rules must be followed:
The different thicknesses of fabric used in the composition of the work must be held together, at first by tacking diagonally across the centre of the piece, then by running stitch all around the piece. Draw the lines on the uppermost cloth. The cutting out must be done little by little, inch by inch with properly sharpened scissors, a few millimetres around the outside of the design. The cut edge of this first piece of cloth is folded back bit by bit to be attached to the second by hemstitch. Each successive thickness should be worked in the same fashion, so that its colours outline the contours of the previous layer.

The more complex the design, the more inlay and appliqué can be used to vary the interplay of colours.

The Hawaiian Islands

Captain Cook discovered the Polynesian archipelago in 1778. Not long after, Hawaiian quilting was born in Honolulu, with the first lessons in patchwork given to the native women by English missionaries. They learnt to sew together the small scraps of cloth the thrifty missionaries had saved and brought with them. When these 'scrap-bags' ran out, the Hawaiians, having quickly taken to the technique, cut their patches from whole new cloth.

They are inspired by natural forms—breadfruit trees, Barbary figs, pineapples, forget-me-nots, and some mythical motifs that were once royal insignia. There are the characteristic garlands of these islands, called *leis*. Originally the colours were a vivid red on a white background (the red Pai Ula motif). Then appeared bright green on a white ground, specially appropriate for all the motifs inspired by plants and trees. Red and bright yellow, the Hawaiian royal colours, became favourites. The original feature of Hawaiian quilts is their use of a large central motif cut out of a single sheet, covering the whole of the backcloth.

These quilts are generally done in reverse appliqué, which is to say that the white cloth is cut out and then hemstitched to the brightly-coloured background piece, letting the motif show through from the second layer. They generally measure $2{\cdot}10 \times 1{\cdot}90$ m. Their quilting follows the outline of the design in expanding rows.

North America

Perhaps we should remember here that America's famous patchwork style really combines two techniques—appliqué and adjoining patchwork.

Here, though, we are only going to talk about appliqué patchwork, and quilts in particular. The technique has been employed for economy's sake since the dawn of time; each still good piece of a discarded garment or any other fabric in everyday use was cut out to be reused alongside many other patches chosen for the same reason. Rearranging these motley fragments, juggling with shapes and colours, gave birth not only to attractive cloth, but eventually to real works of art. A great source of free material was the legendary scrap-bag or bit-bag, filled with

Hawaiian quilt, leaf design in natural colours. Aliette Texier collection.

'The wide world of patchwork'.
Old quilts from North America.
Le Rouvray collection.

Left: *Note the edging of little triangles in the two colours of the 'blocks'.*

Below: *Bouquet motifs. Note the quilting around them.*

morsels of cloth from the household or offcuts from clothes-making. Dutch and British emigrants to North America before 1800 encountered many cash difficulties due to the high price of imported manufactured goods, importable only by voyages that were still long, arduous and relatively infrequent. Around this time the scrap-bag therefore became an important household item, and little by little this recycling technique grew from a habit into a fashion and at last a tradition.

The underlying inspiration was geometrical and repetitive. Each motif, made up of several pieces, formed a block. This basic motif was then repeated over a background to create the characteristic patchwork quilt (usually more like a thick coverlet or counterpane than Continental *duvets* or British down-filled quilts). One exception to this generally geometric tradition is 'crazy-patch', in which appliqué patches are distributed like a mosaic, just as they come; the joins are often embellished with a bright embroidery stitch (chain stitch, herringbone stitch, cross stitch and closed herringbone stitch).

19

Old North American quilt.
Edging of little triangles in one of the colours from the central
design. Le Rouvray collection.

Collectors devoted to unusual art forms have recognised the true
value of these marvellous things, created to meet the simplest
everyday need, and they hang them on walls to be admired as
purely decorative tapestry. Appliqué techniques have changed
little, but their scope has widened until today all kinds of themes,
figurative or otherwise, have been adapted into adventurous new
art forms, paintings in textiles.

Classic American block patterns.
From top to bottom and left to right:
Prairie Flower; Lobster; Bridal Wreath;
Tulip Crib; Oak Leaf; Tulip Design;
Pomegranate; Poinsettia (or Flower of
Christmas); Wild Rose; Hearts and
Flowers; The Melon;
The Rose of Sharon.

22

Classic American blocks based on geometric forms: star and tree-of-life patterns.
From top to bottom and left to right: *Star of Le Moyne; French Star; Missouri Star (or Shining Star);*
Virginia Star; Enigma Star; Falling Star (or Circling Swallow, or Flying Star, or Flying Swallow);
St.-Louis Star; Blazing Star; Pierced Star; Pine Tree; Temperance Tree; Forbidden-Fruit Tree.

Below: *Look at how several block designs are used and arranged on this old original quilt. The edge motif*
harmonizes with the whole, perfectly complementing it. Le Rouvray collection.

Tools and materials

Make a point of collecting all the tools you will need before you begin. Some things will already be in most needlework boxes:
Good slender scissors for thin delicate fabrics.
Stronger scissors (or dressmaking shears) for cutting out cardboard templates or thick cloth.
A good supply of sewing needles will save you much tearing of hair.
A thimble (!).
Pins with large coloured heads for securing the patches, and very thin steel pins, to avoid leaving holes in some very fine fabrics.
Tacking (basting) thread.
Sewing thread. Ideally you should have an assortment of colours to match the various fabrics you will be using. If you cannot quite

run to this, at least have a supply of white and black thread, white for all the light colours and black for the darker ones. And remember that in adding a light piece to a darker one, your seam will be less visible if you use dark thread.

A spool of silk thread, if you are planning to use real silk.

Embroidery thread, if you would like to attach and surround your patches with embroidered seams that are meant to be seen.

A tape measure to help you work out the proportions for laying out designs over large surfaces such as coverlets or wall-hangings. As well as this sewing material you should also have an iron and pressing-cloth to hand.

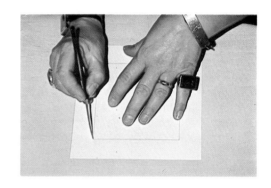

Then, for the design aspects of the craft:

Tracing paper.

A graduated rule.

A roll of sticky tape.

A black pencil and dressmaker's chalk, the pencil for making out light cloth and the chalk for dark cloth.

Cardboard, to make templates out of: bristol board, or bits of card (packaging, old exercise-book covers, old notepads, box-tops and so on). I also recommend graph paper (squared paper) which can make drawing templates for small geometric figures so much easier. The majority of traditional patchwork motifs are made up of such geometric shapes—squares, triangles, lozenges, circles, pentagons, octagons, hexagons. Geometric templates are commercially available. Finally, to make cutting out templates easier, find yourself a sharp craft-knife, scalpel or cutter, a special tool using razor blades.

I wouldn't be surprised if you could find most of this already somewhere round the house!

You can see from the photographs how useful the craft-knife is for cutting out—without ragged edges—a cardboard frame to help you centre a motif accurately.

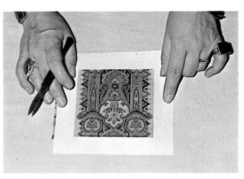

Choosing your materials

The 'scrap-bag', which I prefer to call the 'treasure-chest', with old clothes, old ties and scraps of material.

Of course the American scrap-bag, long famous among lovers of patchwork, has long ago solved all the problems. It was at once simple and difficult; you had only the leftovers of what had already been used around the house, and you had to be content with that and know how to get the best out of it. And these scraps, having 'matured', gave the finished patchwork a wholly inimitable warmth and range of textures.

It is also great fun to rummage through old attics and cupboards, your grandparents', your friends', or simply your own. You can make the most extraordinary discoveries, styles and textures with that indefinable period charm —not to mention such refinements as pillow-lace twirled around cushions by superlatively able hands that did not know the meaning of haste. And if you can find no such treasures of your own (or by getting them from your friends!) there are always second-hand shops, market stalls, jumble sales and charity shops to delight you.

But we should not forget that some of the appliqué works whose particular character we have looked at in preceding chapters are made out of new cloth. Fabric shops are always selling off remnants and off-cuts. So, even if you have no handy bit-bag, you can be sure of good results by buying small pieces of just the texture and colour your project demands.

Which only goes to prove that nothing is impossible!

However, you should choose your cloth carefully by one set of criteria, and those are the uses to which your masterpiece is going to be put.

'Even the smallest scraps are useful.' A mosaic of old scraps of printed cloth found in a country attic.

26

Preparing the cloth

If you want to make something for everyday use, it is going to have to be washable, and in such a way that none of its various bits will shrink, stretch, or shed dye all over their neighbours. This can happen even to so-called 'washable' fabrics on their first contact with water. That is why, as a general rule, you must wash and iron every single piece before you use it.

For wall-hangings or other decorative objects that can be left to the dry-cleaners, it will be enough to steam the pieces—go over them with a warm iron and damping-cloth, smoothing out anything crumpled.

Lace gone dusty or yellowed by age can be cleaned with a weak solution of soap or gentle detergent in warm water. Leave the pieces to soak only a short time in this solution, which, old and fragile as they are, may otherwise chew them up. Rinse them thoroughly and lay them out flat to dry, pinned down. If the lace is not dirty, simply moisten it and dry it the same way.

If you choose a geometric composition, perhaps on the lines of the American patterns of the 'golden age' of patchwork, you should preserve its unity by using the same material throughout.

Cottons

This is the most popular fabric, because it has all the necessary qualities—it is easy to cut, it holds pleats and folds, it does not change shape thanks to its generally fine and close-woven texture, it does not slip and frays little (if at all). You have a very wide choice of cotton-based fabrics—Liberty cottons, Indian cottons, Provençal-style cottons, poplins, chintzes, cretonnes, ginghams. A thicker variety, piqué, is less easy to work with, but its body and ribbed appearance, reminiscent of old-fashioned quilting, make it the ideal backcloth for coverlets.

Large centrepiece or napkin in cotton edged with bias binding, and quilted all over. Le Rouvray collection.

Two original designs in which Michèle David happily unites witty design with the subtle effects of monochrome and matt fabrics.

Linen

This gives rather open textures, which can cause some problems because the looser the weave the faster it frays. It makes very attractive backgrounds for wall-hangings. Also, you can cut appliqué patches directly out of it, without any turnover at the edge; it will fray between the stitches, giving a naive, spontaneous look to your design—though you would be wise not to make anything that will be washed or handled frequently this way. A wall-hanging that need only be dry-cleaned, however, would be fine. As a background, hessian, which comes in an attractive range of colours, has the advantage of being cheap.

Velvet

This can be plain or ribbed. As fine or broad-ribbed corduroy, it can be salvaged from trousers or children's clothes. There it comes in all the colours of a child's wardrobe, and in consistent quality. The direction of the ribbing can play an important part in your design. Who wouldn't be tempted to use chestnut-coloured corduroy to represent a ploughed field? Or who could resist using these regular rows of thin or thicker lines for a 'log-cabin' design? (The so-called 'log-cabin' is a classic American motif made up of strips arranged around a little central square, meeting along the diagonals to create an optical effect well known to patchwork lovers. A single square of this kind will make a very pretty cushion. And several cushions of this kind in different shades of a single colour will very discreetly liven up a plain settee.)

Smooth velvets are of interest for their literally velvety texture, for the depth of their shades, and for the special effects you can

In this design by Germaine Barthélemy, the dress is in velvet. Note also the use of lace for neck and sleeves, and braid for the hairstyle. The jewellery is real.

create by exploiting the depth of their pile. The same piece can give you very different intensities of tone, letting you double the number of shades in a monochrome composition. Keep control of the direction of the pile, and this subtle effect will bring you interesting results! Do not forget that velvet must be ironed on the back, with a damping-cloth, and that crumples can be removed simply by hanging the piece over the steam from a pan of boiling water. It is best to iron velvet by rubbing the wrong side across the face of an upright steam iron, so that the pile is not depressed at all, or by using a special velvet ironing pad, available from good department stores. Velvet is a delicate material, and quite hard to work with because almost anything leaves a mark on it—a pin, tacking, an iron. . . Be careful!

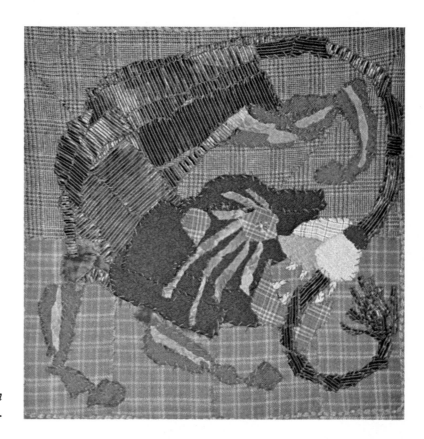

Chica. How to put new life into well-worn tweeds.

Woollens

Their textures and variety of appearance are their special strengths, however different their fibres, weaves or thicknesses. Their most outstanding qualities are warmth and 'presence'. The thickest of them are of course hard to work into appliqué form, but the graininess of tweeds, the lines of herringbone tweed, the bias of serge—to mention only a few of the many varieties—are extra factors which can enrich a composition in cloth. It can also be an advantage to choose woollens for a coverlet which will double as an extra blanket at night. Many worn-out men's clothes in fine woollens can be used as appliqués, geometric or otherwise, against a backcloth of thick wool, adding to their decorative qualities that extra warmth so valuable in a rather cool countrified bedroom. In a decorative hanging the judicious choice of a thick wool element in the design can double its effect, by contrast with flatter or cooler neighbouring elements.

30

*Chica. A work of a rare, strangely atmospheric and poetic quality.
Coarse woven wool backcloth, with finer or coarser wool appliqué.*

Felt

Thanks to its unwoven texture it can be cut and sewn directly, without leaving turnovers round the edge of each piece; the range of colours is very wide. Better still, it comes in wide (180cm) widths, which allows you to make large textile pictures on a seam-free background. To put felt appliqué into place quickly, you can even use a special fabric glue. However, if you want a creation durable enough to be dry-cleaned you should sew on each patch, because the dry-cleaning chemicals will dissolve those glues, and you risk being left with a bare background and a handful of felt fragments!

Felt appliqué fish. Marie-Janine Solvit.

Silks

These lend themselves, understandably, to refined and delicate designs. Think of those marvellous Indian scarves, still in fashion, whose myriad designs can enrich a composition and whose patterns can enhance plain silks. Always sew on your silk patches with various shades of silk thread. The fineness of the material will suffer if you grudge it this well-earned luxury. It will also oblige you to get it an adequate lining to make up for its thinness and transparency. Do not forget that *silk is ironed dry*, with a warm iron, and that it must never be ironed moist like cotton; any piece ironed wet may end up looking like an irremovable grease-stain. You will notice that the foldovers around your appliqué patches show through the silk's transparency. They must be folded back only a few millimetres, therefore, and the finished piece will remain very fragile.

J. Le Voyer. The spirit of Brittany, in silk.

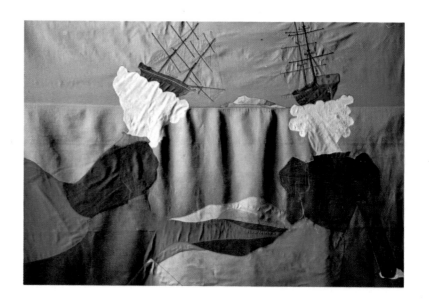

Satins

Characterized by their brightness, they do not exactly fit into traditional patchwork styles, but, like some other glossy fabrics, They lend themselves very well to the revival of Twenties fashions. They are fairly delicate to work with, and stay fragile in the finished piece, the least brush against something being likely to pull loose a thread and spoil the smooth-skinned effect. They should be banished from everything in everyday use, coverlets or any other piece of movable household furnishing. At least, that's what I think. . . .

J. Le Voyer. You will recognise the centre of this appliqué panel from the cover of this book.

33

Marc Tardy. Three Trees. Net and leather appliqué on a woollen backcloth.

Ribbons, bias bindings, fringes . . .

These will go very well as edgings in geometric designs. They come in all widths, colours, textures; add to that a wide choice of decorated ribbons, and you will see how very interesting they can be in appliqué. Depending on the style of your piece, you can choose them either matt or glossy. They are very easy to put on. They need no turnover, of course. But the broadest ones can be cut into little geometric shapes—squares, rectangles, lozenges and so on. Some can divide a backcloth into squares in which you can put appliqué motifs. You can create an American quilt effect this way relatively quickly.

Do not overlook bias bindings, either; they come in a lively choice of colours, and by their weave can adapt themselves to all the curves and convolutions your imagination can come up with.

Binding and webbing, in addition to their decorative qualities, can be sewn to the upper edges and back of a wall hanging, so a wooden batten can be slipped through to give it 'invisible' stiffening. They are also useful for strengthening the base fabric where the hooks to hang it up will be sewn on.

Paule Bassat. Trees made of lace heighten the impression of moonlight.

Trimmings

Their particular relief effects will enliven your work—pompoms, tassels, cords. . . You may think them rather too fragile, but if you have sewn them solidly onto your backcloth they will emerge from dry-cleaning unscathed. Remember that all they need is a little encouragement to show you all their tremendous sense of fun! Cords, from the thinnest to the fattest, can be important elements in a mural design relying heavily on relief effects.

Lace

Lacework is presently recapturing the place it has always deserved in our affections. The presence of lace in an appliqué design can bring it undeniable charm and refinement. Depending on where you place it, and its importance in the whole design, it can create an air of gaiety, antiquity, mystery, translucency, romance or simplicity. On page 27 I have given some suggestions for restoring old lace. If your design depicts a room with a window, large or small, try giving it real lace curtains; I leave you to enjoy the delicacy of the result and the relief effect this precious material can give.

Geneviève Barthélemy. The collars are lace, with white ric-rac around the curtains.

Michèle Bedel de Raffin. Private collection. Marvellous composition in sparkling fabrics.

Marc Tardy. Handbag with relief appliqué in leather.

Lamés and sparkling fabrics

This is another family of materials you will not find in traditional appliqué work, but in the unbridled world of contemporary art they appear frequently. There is nothing better for conjuring up an aura of festivities, lights, enchanted evenings. This is why you should not leave them out of your bit-bag or your designs, and you will see just how much the smallest scrap of lamé or other glittering fabric can heighten a whole design by itself.

Skins, leathers, hides

The glossy or velvet textures of this material can enrich an appliqué piece by its own special presence. We have seen it in Central European costume, and we come back to it now in modern creations. Do not be afraid of using skins, with or without fur; unless they are extremely thick they are easier to work with than you might think. Special needles (leather needles) are recommended to avoid tearing the skin when sewing.

Buttons

These are hardly ever found in traditional embroidered appliqué work. On the other hand, they are an important feature of many modern designs, to which they add relief, colour and texture at the same time. No doubt many will turn up among the debris of your bit-bag. However, you are advised not to use them on a coverlet which is often sat on, or at least only to use them as occasional reinforcements on material soft and thick enough to swallow them up out of the way of all possible snags! On the other hand, buttons on a wall-hanging can become fruit in the trees, the centres of flowers, animals' eyes, exotic birds' plumage, stars in the sky and so on.

Finally, all the odd accessories of dressmaking—buckles, press-fasteners, rings, rivets or spangles—should be welcomed. They can tellingly—or humorously—pick out a figure's dress, or provide the metallic elements of a scene (grilles, well chains, balconies and so on), bringing to a technically traditional appliqué that living touch which demonstrates its creator's quest for original expression.

Germaine Barthélemy. Notice the use of buttons to contrast with the muted plaid of the bird's body.

Choosing and arranging your subjects

Blocks and quilts

Appliqué technique lends itself to thousands of different concepts and styles. The great era of American appliqué quilts has bequeathed us a whole range of block designs which have become classics, each with its own name and intended to be reproduced as often as necessary to bring the particular background to life.

American appliqués were almost always quilts, coverlets or counterpanes, designed to cover wooden beds from head to foot in the 19th-century manner, and fall past the mattress on either side. Their dimensions tended to be less than for our modern divans, which may have neither head nor foot but still need a length of 2·40 to 2·70 metres—depending on whether they cover the pillows or not—by a breadth of 1·60 metres for a single and 2·70 metres for a double bed!

If you decide to try making a quilt, you should choose its design according to the size of the bed, the furnishings around it and the colours already present in the room.

Arranging the motifs

Together we can explore the many permutations possible with a simple geometric shape such as this oval. The more you add, the more animated the design becomes, and the more fun the game. Imagine the infinity of patterns you could build up just by playing around like this with many different shapes in combination! I leave the pleasures of finding out to you.

For regular repetition of a design, lay out the blocks on a gridwork marked onto the backcloth. This can be left showing on the finished piece (if in appliqué, embroidery or similar), or can be tacked (basted) in with thread, which is then removed after the blocks are in place, leaving only the regularly decorated surface. But it is equally authentic to centre a single large motif on the backcloth, such as the *Star of Bethlehem* block, or to lay out some blocks in a circle around the central motif, or in corners around a central rosette. In traditional appliqué there is no asymmetry.

Size of the motifs

On a quilt, for example, the bed size will play a part in this choice; a large central motif will be better adapted to the broad expanse of a double bed. The quilt will assume different shapes, depending on whether it covers a flat mattress, mattress with pillows, pillows plus bolster and so on, and should consequently be differently decorated... The same motif can be reproduced on a larger or smaller scale, tailored not only to the size of the bed but also its prominence in the room. This is an important consideration! Whether the bed is the centrepiece of the room, or whether it cowers timidly in a corner, will determine whether the quilt is

'... as often as necessary to bring the particular background to life.'

Old American quilt.
Le Rouvray collection.

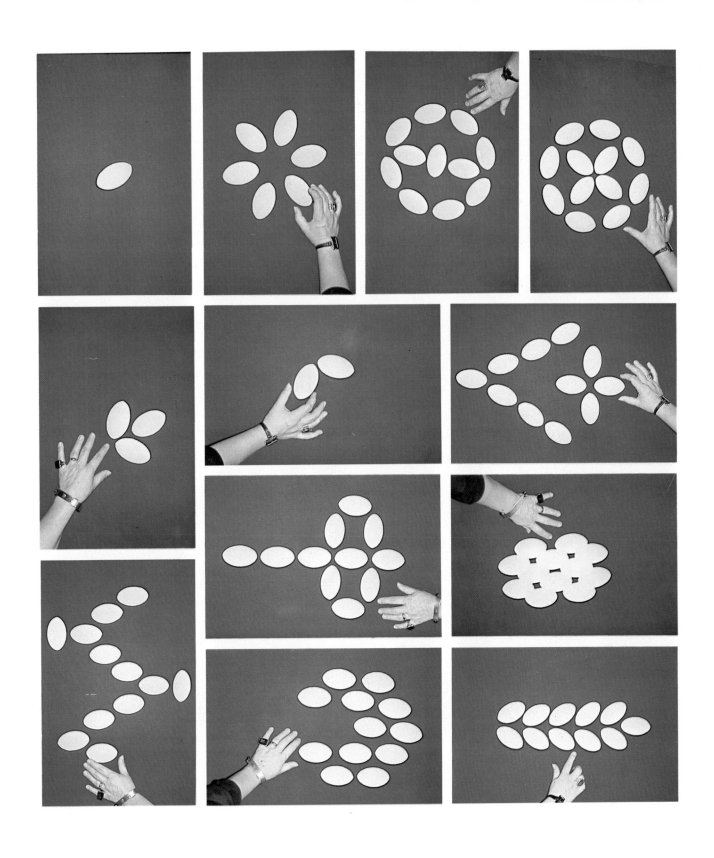

Finding the many permutations possible with a simple geometric shape.

39

The classic American Star of Bethlehem.
Each point of this star is a lozenge-shaped block made up of 49 smaller lozenges. The effect of arrows pointing in towards the centre is easily created by juxtaposing two lozenges of the same colour.

40

supposed to dominate the decor or shrink humbly into the background. Not that it should be blotted out; it ought rather to keep a quiet presence of its own.

As a general rule—large motifs on large beds, little ones on small beds. But all the same, everyone must trust their own taste; some large quilts with very small geometric designs are marvels that would look good anywhere, and a great 'Tree of Life' centred on a single bed can make an excellent artistic effect.

Style of the motifs

Judicious mixing and blending is possible. Of course, you will not want to choose a heavily romantic motif to go with Jacobean furniture, any more than an ultramodern design to go with Regency suites. Above all, no Hawaiian breadfruit trees alongside a piece of Chinese laquerwork or austere geometric patterns flanking Louis XV chairs. I am giving you examples of obviously extreme incompatibility, but many traditional appliqué quilt styles, most often those made up of groups of plain geometric figures, will fit without serious difficulty into a very wide range of furnishings.

The more sober and starkly simple the furniture (Jacobean, Spanish, American, Colonial, 'farmhouse' and other rustic styles, bamboo and rattan, and most modern styles) the better it takes to a decorated quilt. The more sophisticated and elaborate the style (gildings, flutings, whorls and extravagances) the more it needs to have what goes with it carefully selected.

The different elements of one design must not harm each other, clash, or look wearyingly alike. Where walls are brightly coloured or heavily decorated, you should go for an airy design picking up a dominant colour from the walls; you might even reproduce a design from the wallpaper in appliqué, but freed from its surroundings and in a suitably contrasting colour to your backcloth. For walls painted to match the curtains, you could get some of the curtain material, cut out bits of the pattern and resew them as appliqué on a quilt backcloth; space them out more, so as not to look jumbled when all three things (walls, quilt, curtains) are seen together.

Evidently, then, unless you are dealing with a plain, bare, unfurnished room, you will have to consider its character and style when planning your appliqué. Think it out well in advance, to leave yourself as little room as possible for regrets afterwards.

Traditional patchworks on American Colonial furniture. Aliette Texier collection.

J. Le Voyer. Blue appliqués in cold tones.

Oxanne. Warm tones.

Colour pictures

This particular kind of appliqué design is best suited to a room with plain, uncomplicated decor, which will tend to make it stand out better. Hence my own preference for walls in one quiet colour against which other things can assert themselves properly. It is certainly hard to imagine a multicoloured wall-hanging against wallpaper with an equally motley pattern. A very wide plain frame would be needed to separate one from the other properly, and it could never be more than a second-best solution. On the other hand, against a white or cream wall avoid backgrounds that are too light; the surface of your hanging may be hard to make out against the wall.

Colour vision is said to trigger off an advance-recoil response, cold colours (the blue to violet range) advancing and warm colours (the red to green range) recoiling. Cold colours are also considered restful and warm colours stimulating. Medical authorities have gone to the length of advising a choice of colours precisely tailored to a patient's problems—violet for manics, red for depressives, yellow for listlessness. So that is how important colour choice can be! The way they coincide can also affect them. Take blue, for example; beside it a red looks more violet, a yellow greener, and white will take on a slight blue tinge itself.

On the other hand, if you care to try colouring the many patches of an appliqué design differently, you will soon see that the basic design and composition change drastically according to the colours you choose and their respective positions. It can therefore be interesting to make 'dry runs' with coloured paper or even the fabrics themselves. Three general types of colour scheme are open to you:

1. 'Cameo', or monochrome, which involves using a single dominant colour in a wide range of tones, shades and gradations.

2. Contrasted, which involves using bright colours. Superimposition makes each one stand out spectacularly in contrast to the others, in an explosion of colour (as, for example, in the Fon appliqués and the *molas*).

3. Subtly shaded, which involves balancing the complimentary effects of soft or pastel colours, the use of compound colours (or fabrics such as Liberty cottons, whose very fine patterns will tend to make the eye merge their component colours), and exploiting their varying degrees of softness or strength and their mutual effects.

The orientation of a room can influence the choice of colours; a room darkened by facing north can be cheered up by the warmth of reds, oranges and yellows; and the presence of blues, greens and violets can soften the sometimes fatiguing intensity of too direct sunlight. Here we should remember the amazing extent to which you can transform the lighting and atmosphere of a room by juggling with its colour scheme. But some people will prefer the tranquil heaviness of a bluish shadowy room, whereas others will prefer the sun-sparkling energy of warm colours.

There is only one more essential: avoid muddling the colours by mistaken superimpositions—doing that in a design demands a certain coherency of style. But because every piece we make is a special case (and for that we can never be too grateful!) it must conform to its creator's own tastes. So to me the supreme rule seems to be: do what seems good to you, and cheerfully follow your own guiding light!

Chica. Subtly shaded.

Michèle David. Blue monochrome on an earth-toned backcloth.

43

Germaine Barthélemy. Contrasted.

44

Making an appliqué, step by step

Now we are ready to work through the creation of a wall-hanging by traditional techniques, step by step.

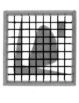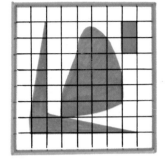

Preparing the templates

First, I draw my landscape directly onto white card (or very stiff paper) to the exact dimensions I want for the finished hanging. If I wanted to reproduce a larger or smaller drawing or other picture, I would use the so-called 'square technique' to enlarge or shrink it to the size I want. This is done by dividing the sketch into squares, then redrawing the grid larger or smaller and copying the design into the squares bit by bit.

I then trace the design onto tracing paper of the same size, which I keep carefully as my key to reconstruct the landscape I am about to turn into a jigsaw. I do this by cutting the white card up very carefully along the lines of my drawing. The pieces will become patterns or templates for the various patches of my appliqué. Then, using the tracing, I reassemble them, making the job easier by holding them to each other with small strips of sticky tape.

Choosing the fabrics

Since I want to give the scene the light of a sunset, I keep the lighter warm-toned fabrics for the side still sunlit, and darker, cold-toned cloth for the shadowy side. Whites and raw silks will make the outlines of village buildings stand out. What I choose for each patch depends both on what I have available and on my own taste. Because my scrap-bag—I prefer to call it my 'treasure-bag'—contains some pieces of Liberty cotton and other cottons with a small flower pattern, I shall scatter them around freely. You can do the same, provided your chosen design does not demand you reproduce colours faithfully—as it would, for example, if you were reproducing a painting or anything else with proper shading.

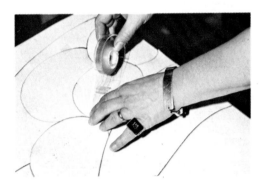

Cutting and fitting the background

My landscape has a very pale blue sky, but the road leading from the foreground to the village should be depicted by the backcloth. I am therefore going to make a two-part backcloth, the lower half in pinkish beige wool and the upper part in very pale blue wool. The two cloths are joined by a straight seam, opened up with iron and damping cloth to make a neat smooth background. Over this I lay out my reconstructed scene, arranging the seam so that it passes behind the houses; the beige can then reappear as the church square and the roads leading off to right and left.

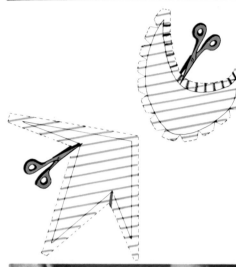

Cutting and laying out the patches

Now I lay out my fabrics side by side to select where they will go, relative to each other. I then detach one of the 'jigsaw' pieces, slicing the tape linking it to its neighbours with a craft-knife or something equally sharp. This will be a piece of grassland. I turn the template over onto the back of a green fabric spotted with small flowers and cut all around it, leaving a margin of about 1·5cm. This border will be folded back over the card outline, the cloth being folded front to back to keep the exact shape. Clip (or notch) the seam allowances around curves and corners so that the edges may be properly turned. I then press in the fold with iron and damping cloth. I let it cool and remove the template, keeping only the patch, now ready for sewing on. I take the next piece off the puzzle, letting a pinkish beige road surface appear; I lay my first patch in place and secure it with a few pins.

I go on to prepare all the patches this way. You can see me putting the second in place, still with pins. The round silhouettes of the trees on the right let the sunny hillside appear between them, so I put this whole patch, yellow with small flowers, on next in one whole piece, and then add the tree patches on top. I continue putting them on like this. The landscape is beginning to take shape! All I need do now is add the trees at left, the cloudy streaks in the sky, and the village houses.

All my hillsides are in Liberty cottons or dark fabric with small flowers. The round light-green trees are cut from one piece of coloured linen. The cypresses to the left of the church came from the woven border of one of my husband's handkerchiefs, and the other trees are various shades of green socks that I split behind the leg and along the sole, then flattened vigorously with iron and cloth. Old ties supplied the trees. The building walls were assorted bits of old summer trousers. The roofs restored some *raison d'être* to a solitary old red kid glove, except for the central one, whose granite red came from an old club tie. The church porch was maroon kid. Finally, poplin from my sons' old shirts, supplied the clouds. And by now each and every piece is in place! Each piece in turn is now hemstitched to the background.

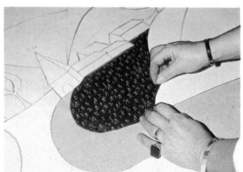

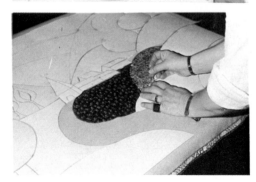

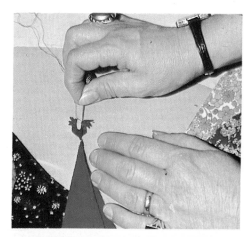

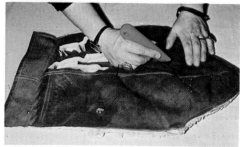

Details

I will now be able to put a little life into the scene by adding one or two details and reliefs; here is a tie offering us some small coloured rosettes. Let's cut it up! The design is too tiny to be flattened out with iron and cloth. I therefore have to fold the fabric bit by bit as I hemstitch it on. And there is my stained-glass window for the church! But it still doesn't look complete without a little felt weathercock silhouette on top of the spire. . .

Among my treasure-trove I find the sleeves of a child's sheepskin coat. On the skin side I draw sheep outlines with a ball-point pen and cut around them with a craft-knife. Cutting them out like this is necessary to keep the pile of the fleece; the technique is useful for any kind of fur. Once the skin is pierced, the hairs separate without being clipped away by the passing blade. My sheep may safely graze in the foreground, at left; I hold back their fleece with my left hand to hemstitch on the skin, having first slipped legs of light kid behind them in such a way that the stitching will hold them on too. The nearest sheep have a bell around their necks (very nice buttons from a bodice). The more distant sheep do not have them; I have made them smaller to heighten the effect of distance.

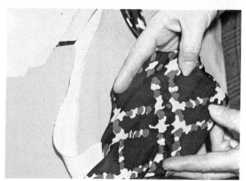

The beiges and ochres on the black ground of this silk tie will be perfect for spotting the two little cows I have let into the light green field at right. The intricacy of cutting out this silk makes me work a little differently; the fabric, laid flat on the background, is sewn on with a tight buttonhole stitch in black thread.

The maroon leather of my husband's old glove will be perfect for cutting out the shape of a cart, and the wheel will stand out better if I put it on leather-side up. I would like to break up the flatness of the beige road a little, too. Some little natural wood beads sewn here and there make good pebbles, getting progressively smaller as the road shrinks in the distance.

Do you know how to make a perfectly straight fold around the edge of your piece? Draw a line across the back with a ruler,

47

using black pencil on light fabrics and white dressmaker's chalk on dark. Put pins along it at regular intervals. Turn the fabric over and fold it along the line, going from one pin to the next. Here I have edged the top half with a small regular running stitch thread, while the other sides were held in place by a sock stitch done from the back.

And here at last is my finished hanging!

Six regular motifs.
Detail of an appliqué quilt.
Le Rouvray collection.

Preparing a corner fold on a patch,
holding it in place with sticky tape before
ironing it in.

Other traditional techniques

The traditional technique followed in the preceding pages demands that every card patch be replaced by its exact duplicate in cloth throughout the composition.

This technique seems to be necessary when the piece is made up of differently-shaped sections that have to link up with each other to the nearest mm or so. But you can manage much more quickly by cutting out each piece with a constant 2 to 3mm margin, letting you judge the necessary foldback by eye, and without using an iron. The cotton used will hold a fold well enough, even if only made between the fingers and reinforced by running a fingernail hard along it. The needle can slip under the cloth to make it fold back.

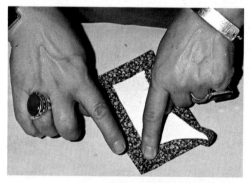

Put all the pieces carefully into place with pins, or, better, with tacking thread which will not slip out—valuable if the task is a long one. Once this is done, sew on each patch step by step.

This technique is most useful for making quilt patterns from the classic American repertoire, or similar designs using semi-abstract arrangements of geometric forms. But if the templates contain many complex curves or other irregularities, the first technique will get you much more precise results. You must also remember that experience plays a considerable part, and that a first attempt is bound to feel hard, while everything will come marvellously right after a little practice. But isn't that always the case?

And here, in a few photos, is a breakdown of the so-called *Snowflake* technique—instant designs on paper, then on cloth.

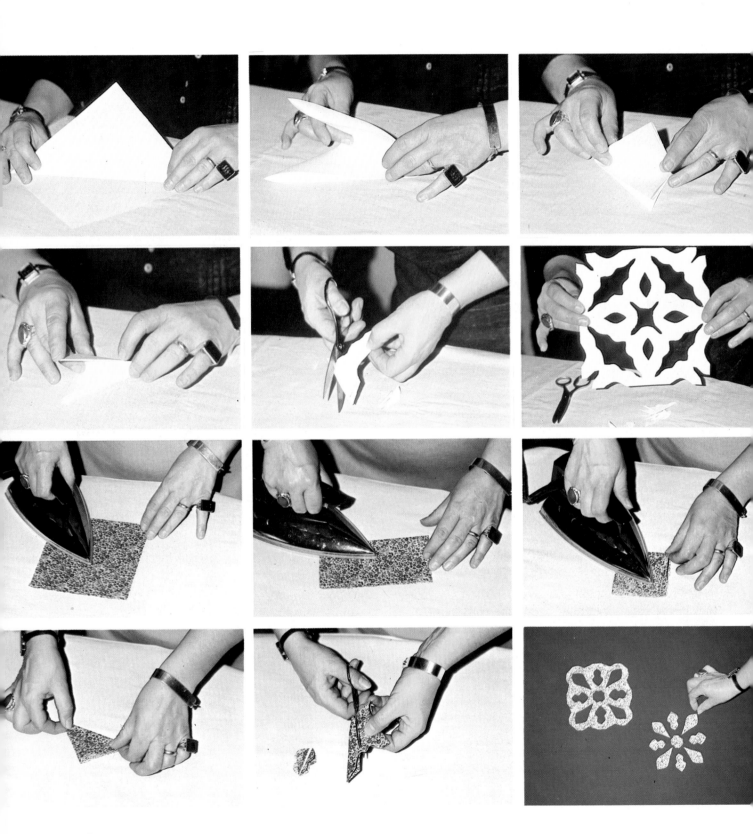

Simplified techniques

These are currently popular with contemporary craftworkers making one-off pieces, mostly 'textile paintings', and cutting out the elements of these directly, without a foldover around them.

On the sewing machine

Some of them put these elements together with a zigzag stitch on a sewing machine, others with satin stitch, to secure the appliqué patch, hide its cut edge and stop the fabric fraying. The elements are initially held in place with tacking stitches, and the sewing machine secures them along a path leading directly from each patch to the next, and thus necessarily using a single colour of thread for the whole work. The intervention of the machine therefore takes away some of the charm of handiwork; the gain in time is given a regrettable emphasis ... but the artistic qualities seem not to suffer.

I cannot let myself leave out any existing techniques, so I will also remind you that it is possible, again with the machine, to use a lockstitch, running around each piece as close as possible to the folded edge of each patch.

By hand

Even keeping within the traditional bounds of pure handiwork, there are still a number of possible ways which do not involve folding the cloth back around each patch. The deliberate choice of a design using enormous and very apparent hem stitch can enliven the piece with a spontaneous charm like that of naive art. You can also surround your patches, cut 'lifesize', with an embroidery stitch following the outlines of the appliqué. Various stitches lend themselves to this technique:

J. Le Voyer. Appliqué done by satin stitch on a sewing machine.

Paule Bassat. Appliqué done in machine zigzag stitch.

52

Chica. Deliberate choice of very large and visible stitching for a piece.

Buttonhole stitch, worked from left to right. The thread passes under the left thumb, a little back from the edge of the patch, in other words overlapping onto the backcloth. The needle enters over the edge of the patch, the point picks up both thicknesses of cloth, then emerges against the ingoing thread, to its right. Good close stitches and the thickness of the material used will combine to cover the outline of the patch. The hand-sewn edging will leave a trail of little vertical lines surrounded by a corded effect.

Satin stitch, differing from buttonhole stitch in that it is made of coupled vertical stitches, done from left to right and up and down but without any edging around them. These stitches form a kind of beading which will mask the join between the two fabrics by covering them over.

Chain stitch, which follows the outlines of each individual patch, the rounded stitches forming a series of little loops, which will hide the join all the better if they are done in a thick material (embroidery cotton or wool).

Closed herringbone stitch, whose cross should be worked astride the outline of the patch. It is worked from left to right. The needle enters at right, comes out at left, above the outline, then goes down to repeat the action below the line, leaving the thread diagonally across it. This repeated movement forms a series of crossbars.

Herringbone stitch, like chain stitch, follows the line of the outline to be covered. The needle makes a vertical stitch from top to bottom, and the thread held back by the thumb of the left hand passes in a loop under the exit point of the needle. The same action, done to one side and the other of the join between the two fabrics, will cover them with its intertwined zigzag.

There are other embroidery stitches I have no room to mention here. The thread colour can match that of the fabric or contrast with it. This crowning refinement can be further heightened by using a fairly thick embroidery cotton, or wool.

Sophie Campbell. Contrasting colours: sewn with a concealed hemstitch later underlined with a running stitch in black a little way in from the edge of the appliqué.

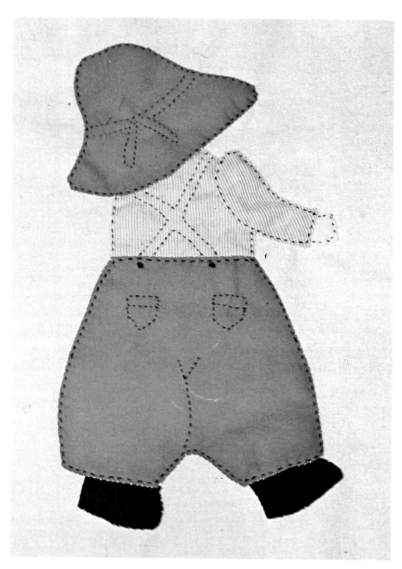

Michèle David. Linen appliqué sewn on with satin stitch, entirely by hand.

Skins and leather

Essentially all the stitches used for appliqué without foldback can equally well be used for skins, leather, kid and so on. A simple running stitch can go round the outline of a leather appliqué, a few millimetres in. However, the thread used should preferably be waxed or strong linen. Special devices for sewing leather can be useful. One can forget the mechanical aspects in giving way to the exceptional charm of the material when well handled. For furs or other skins with hair refer to the technique I used for the sheep (page 47).

Marc Tardy. Leather screen: 'the exceptional charm of the material when well handled'.

Marc Tardy. Handbag. Appliqué with a doll's head and arm emerging in relief from a marvellous leather patchwork.

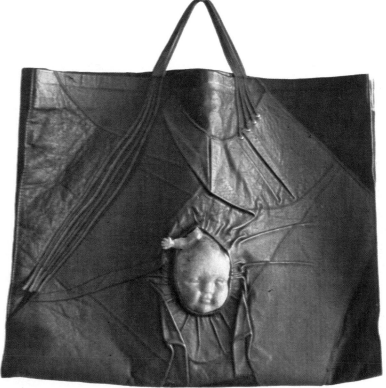

Linings

Useless as a lining almost always is for a decorative wall-hanging, whose backcloth will preserve its surface, it is almost indispensable for some other kinds of work.

A rug

The lining here has two purposes: first, it stops unavoidable friction against the floor wearing away the threads that pass through behind the backcloth. Moreover, its close weave and its weight will make the rug rigid enough to resist rumpling and stop it slipping.

Ideally one should use a sturdy, firmly woven cotton or linen such as twill or duck. Be sure of the quality of your thread, because this kind of work has to survive being trampled underfoot. Allow for a binding, held onto the lining by a firm hemming stitch. The folded-over edge of this should be sewn onto the back; from the front this will give a neat finish with no apparent stitches. You should take care to hold the top onto the lining by some large tacks starting from the centre, to be sure that the two parts are flattened against each other and that no puckers will show up in

Old French prayer mat, appliqué cretonne rectangles. Here the lining is held in by the edging.

Michèle David. Wall hanging. The linen backcloth ensures a completely even surface.

56

Marc Tardy. Lining prevents threads on the back being snagged in use, an important consideration with a handbag.

use. You can also fold over the backcloth of your rug onto the chosen lining material, cut a centimetre or two smaller so that the edge of this foldover can be concealed by the top around it. A tapestry fringe sewn firmly across it on the back will make sure it holds.

Another wise precaution to take before undoing the tacking holding the top onto the lining: separate the fixing points of these two thicknesses from each other, making use of the meeting points of various patches or their geometric centres. If this is not done, it may still go into folds.

Something made of several pieces

(For example: a bag, a cushion, a toy.) The lining will give you a neater finish and hide stitch marks in the backcloth. It should also prevent the threads holding on the appliqués getting hooked onto anything in use.

Clothes

The backcloth will be covered with stitches, so these must inevitably show through at the back. A fine lining will ensure you a neat finish without bulking out the garment.

Michèle Tardy: velvet jacket decorated with appliqués.

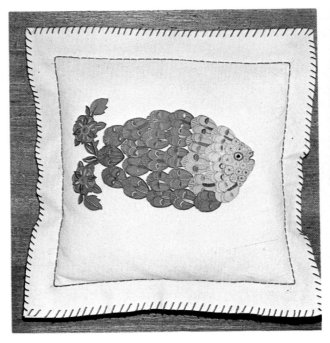

Left: *Madeleine Olive-Dignimont.*
Securing stitches with knots.

Right: *Quilting follows the outlines of the*
motifs. Aliette Texier collection.

Quilting and tie-quilting

A bed-cover on the lines of a traditional American quilt should have three thicknesses—the top (the decorative part); the interior (useful for warmth) and the lining. These have to be held together. You have the choice of two methods, tying or stitching.

Hawaiian quilt. Quilting is done over the
whole background. Aliette Texier
collection.

Tying

This technique involves linking the three thicknesses of cloth by stitches distributed at regular intervals across the design (at the corners or the centre of various patches) and held individually at the back by a solid knot. This technique resembles the mattress stitches on old-fashioned wool mattresses, regularly distributed to ensure a constant thickness of wool over the whole mattress. These knot stitches can become a whole new decorative element if they are worked in a thread colour contrasting with the rest of the piece, or if they emphasize some geometric centres, or if they punctuate some areas.

Quilting

This involves linking the three thicknesses of cloth by hand sewing that follows the outline of each patch, or that decorates the whole surface with square or lozenge shapes bearing no relation to the appliqué design, or even by surrounding the outlines of the appliqué motifs with lines of equidistant stitches (something you often find on Hawaiian quilts).

You should mark out the design chosen for quilting when the piece is still flat with its entire surface visible; that way you will get a better idea of the effect produced. But if, for example, you are dealing with semi-circles in staggered rows—arranged like fishscales—they can be marked out as you go along, your pencil (hard and dry) following the outlines of a single template.

If you want to add quilting between the blocks of your appliqué, you can equally well draw your chosen pattern onto a thin piece of paper pinned to the appropriate place on top of your piece. The needle will go through the paper and the three layers at once. When you have finished, simply pull the paper away gently and the design will appear, faithfully transferred. This refinement of hand oversewing means a little extra work, which should not discourage you, because the result will look marvellous and be wholly faithful to the great tradition.

Choice of thread is important, because it must be solid enough to hold the quilt pattern through three layers of cloth, and must not break when you pull it taut. The best threads for this are silk twist, so-called 'button thread', thin waxed threads (even no. 100, the thinnest, can't be broken by hand!) and also pearl cotton sold in large spools. Avoid ordinary sewing thread absolutely, because it will get entangled and break in the needle's eye.

From time to time do a back-stitch to hold the tension of your thread better. Don't be afraid either of leaving good cut-off knots at the back of the piece, or of good solid anchorages at the end of the seam. Remember that this slow work must stand up to many years of wear.

The left hand should hold up the surface of the cloth, pressing upwards, while the right hand inserts the needle vertically downwards, then sticks it out again a few millimetres further on, following the marked-out design and helping the needle to resurface with an almost automatic movement of the thumb.

There is another quilting technique, traditionally called 'up and down', which involves inserting the needle vertically downwards with the right hand, then forcing it vertically up again a few millimetres further on with the left hand under the piece. With this, though, you must take care to keep an even distance between stitches on the two sides of the piece. This method is most useful for dealing with webbing or other thick cloth. In both cases use a short needle.

Preparation

These two techniques require minute preparation to cut out any risk of imperfections. If you cannot find a large enough table, spread your materials flat on the floor. First spread out the cloth you have chosen for the lining—without any concessions as to quality, because it will be an integral part of your creation and must wear as well as the rest of it. Then cover it with the webbing,

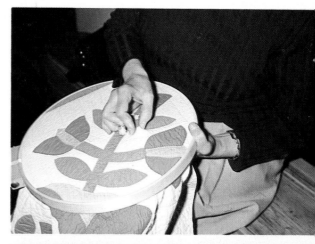

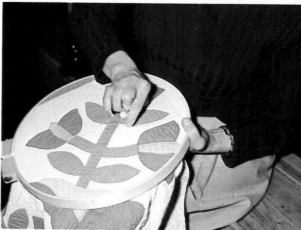

The two actions of quilting. Sophie Campbell.

The lively background created by geometric quilting. Le Rouvray collection.

59

smoothing it out carefully by hand from the centre outwards. Secure the two layers together with large tacking stitches, also radiating outwards from the centre, tracing out a cross in straight thread and an X in diagonals to the corners. Once the first two layers are secure, repeat the same procedure for the decorated top. Don't let any folds creep in between the three layers. Your final success rests on getting it right now!

Two devices are used to make finishing easier—the large frame and the embroidery hoop.

The large frame

This is made of two wooden battens as long as the quilt is wide. At the two ends wooden pegs or metal pins (5 to 10cm long) stick out vertically, fitting into holes in the other two battens making up the other sides of the frame. These pegs keep the rolling battens, the ones with holes, in position. These are wrapped in a roll of webbing, to which the edges of the quilt should be sewn with stitches solid enough so that the cloth thus fixed will both roll off evenly and stand up to being pulled taut.

It is usual to estimate the length of the pegged battens as twice that of your outstretched arm, which will let you reach the centre of the exposed portion of the piece easily enough, whichever of the unrolling bars you are sitting next to.

The ideal height for setting up this foldaway frame (easily made with four battens and two trestles, and easily stored once dismantled) is that of a table, but it also depends on the height of chair used. You must be able to get your knees right under the flat frame and not be too cramped in front, because the position quickly becomes tiring. Commercially available whitewood trestles are not expensive; you can screw the fixed bars of the frame to them, pegs upward, and adapt them to the best chair height later (which you will find by experiment).

As the work advances, you roll up a little of the finished work, at the same time unrolling more of the work from the opposite bar.

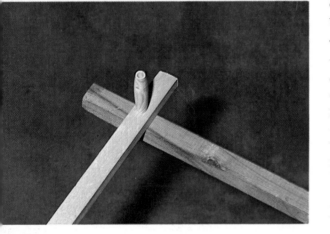

Corner of the large frame.

The embroidery frame

You buy this ready-made. It is generally round, sometimes oval, made of two wooden hoops—one, closed, which can stand on a leg or be clamped to the edge of a table, the other split and fitted with a screw clamp. The portion of the piece you are quilting is placed on the closed hoop. You then push the open hoop down over it and clamp it shut with a few turns of the screw. This leaves the surface of the cloth caught between the two hoops, stretched taut as a drumskin.

This device gives you no vast area to work on, and cannot be used with loosely-woven fabrics because it may stretch them. But traditional quilting is always done on tightly-woven cottons that run no such risk, and these frames have the extra advantage of being far less cumbersome than a large rectangular frame on trestles.

Sophie Campbell, patchwork teacher, busy quilting.

Lastly, in the absence of either of these aids to quilting, you can just hold the three layers together more simply by large numbers of tacking stitches, turning them into a thoroughly solid material, a sufficient density of stitches compensating for the absence of mechanical aids.

The embroidery hoop, showing the small working area.

*Highly decorated border. Early
American quilt. Le Rouvray collection.*

*'With rounded corners'. Aliette Texier
collection.*

*Edging punctuated with lace. Germaine
Barthélemy.*

Borders

These are both an important part of your work's finish and a decorative factor in themselves, as a frame is for a picture. Above all, we are concerned with their importance in the finishing of quilts, whose three layers must be concealed and edge over together. Borderings go from the narrowest—a bias binding sewn across the edge, either straight or in a curved outline with rounded corners—to the widest—a strip of fabric itself appliquéd with motifs related to those in the central design. Old traditional quilts have a huge variety of edge styles.

It can be interesting to repeat one of the elements from the central design, effectively echoing it, and to experiment with various colour contrasts. Only your own creative spirit can decide, taking the whole style of the piece into account. If you opt for a string of appliqué motifs, work out their respective placements very carefully to get an exact symmetry from corner to corner. Then, this precaution taken, put on your edgings and prepare the corners. Fit them very closely to the corners of the quilt before putting your last appliqué motifs over them, which should now mask their 45° cuts. You will centre the last motifs more perfectly following this advice.

Quilts inspired by Hawaiian styles, made with one huge appliqué in a single colour contrasting with that of the backcloth, and cut away to let the design the backcloth makes show through, will not need any extra border. In fact the backcloth should stand out a little all around the cutaway appliqué layer, making a simple border reappearing as overlap. It can be folded back to cover the webbing in the centre, then the lining, slightly inset, can be put over that and sewn on with a simple buttonhole stitch.

Many old quilts were surrounded with a giddy whirl of garlands, festoons, foliage in bias binding, or multicoloured stripes picking up the shades of the central design. Choose, experiment, imagine. You will do it all the more enthusiastically when you consider that at this stage your long task is nearing its end, and you will soon be able to relax and enjoy your masterpiece.

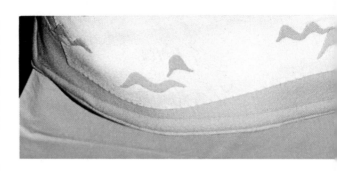

Simple finishing: two rows of stitches between piping creates a corded effect. Marie-Janine Solvit.

Hanging up wall-hangings

There are several ways open to you:

1. If no special preparation is being made for hanging, you can always make the nails in the wall more decorative by fitting each one with a beautiful large bead, fitted round it and held in by the nail-head. Choose the colours of your beads to go with the dominant colours of the hanging.

2. Sew, right along the upper edge of your hanging at the back, a binding left open at both ends for a rod to be slipped in, which you then hold there by sewing up the ends. The drape will be much improved without making the whole thing too rigid.

3. Sew, right along the upper edge of your hanging at the back, a binding or webbing to which you fix, with waxed thread, hanging rings about 10cm apart. Fit x-hook nails along the wall at the level of each ring.

4. Sew, here and there, at the top and back of your hanging, some vertical loops made of small pieces of ribbon, into which you slip a rod which cannot be seen from the front.

5. From the same fabric as the backcloth of the hanging, or in a matching shade, make some large loops fixed between the back and the lining, into which you slip a wooden pin which can then be seen between them. The colour and texture of this pin will also be of some importance. This method of hanging can be particularly attractive when the fabrics used are large matt linens.

Old quilt turned into wall-hanging. Aliette Texier collection.

Chica. We conclude our trip around the world of appliqué with this contemporary piece.

Conclusion

Here ends our trip through the world of appliqués, and the techniques by which they are created. I hope I have been of some help to you, and I wish you as much enthusiasm and as many pleasures as I have found in unveiling for you this fundamentally simple technique—simple, but time-hallowed, for even the ancient Egyptians knew it.

Forgive me the forbidding way I have been laying down the law; I was doing it only to steer you towards a success thorough enough to reward you for your efforts and your patience. I wish you hours of happy creativity.

I will not need to remind you that few other pleasures are a patch on it. . . .